DATE DUE

NOV 20 '91			
DEC 20 '98			
	261-2500		Printed in USA

how to have fun with macrame

By Editors of Creative EDUCATION, INC.

Illustrated by Nancy Inderieden

DEDICATED TO
TOM, MIKE, KRISTY and TIMMY

creative
craft
book

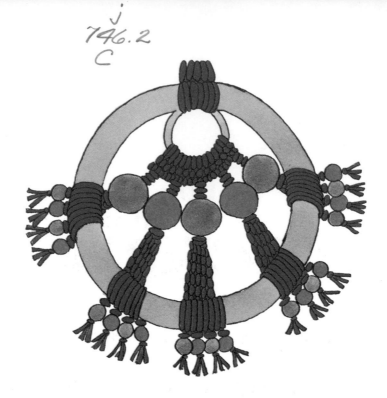

Library of Congress Number: 73-19667
ISBN: 0-87191-290-2

Published by Creative Education, Mankato, Minnesota 56001. Distributed by Childrens Press, 1224 West Van Buren Street, Chicago, Illinois 60607

Library of Congress Cataloging in Publication Data
Creative Educational Society, Mankato, MN
   How to have fun with macrame.
   (Creative craft book)
   SUMMARY: A simple instruction to macrame with instructions for a variety of projects.
1. Macrame—Juvenile literature. (1. Macrame.
2. Handicraft) I. Title.
TT840.C73   746.4   73-19667
ISBN 0-87191-290-2

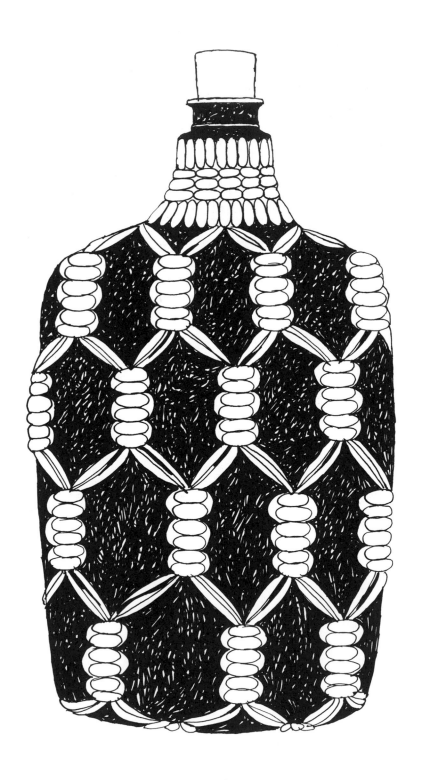

4

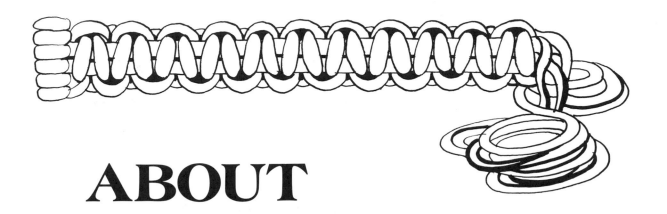

ABOUT MACRAME

Macrame is the ancient craft of tying knots. This craft began thousands of years ago with early man. Knotted cords have been found in ancient Egyptian tombs that are almost 3,500 years old.

Knots were also used for medical purposes very early in history. In the first century A.D. a Greek physician wrote an essay on surgical slings. Many of the knots described and illustrated in this essay are still being used by surgeons today.

Sailors carried the craft of tying knots all over the world. Not only did they use knots to fasten their sails but they spent many of the long hours on board ship tying knots. The cords they knotted were used as a fringe or border on clothing and decorative items such as wall hangings.

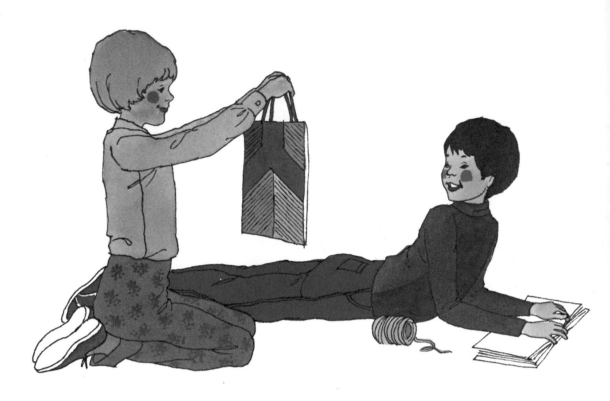

During the 18th Century the art was forgotten. It was no longer used for decorations or clothing. Lace had now been introduced. But, in the 19th Century sailors started knotting belts, purses, hammocks, rugs, and covered bottles. When they would reach a port they would sell or trade these items. Their products became very popular. Soon other people were trying to learn this art.

Today this ancient craft is called Macrame. It is very easy to learn and very popular as a hobby for young people. Many beautiful wall hangings, belts, purses, and other decorative articles can be made by tying these knots.

LET'S BEGIN

To begin you must have a few special supplies. You will need "T" pins. If you do not know what a "T" pin is, look at the illustration. These pins will be used to pin down your macrame cords.

A foam rubber pillow makes a very nice macrame board. If you pin your macrame cord to the pillow to hold it, it will be easier for you to work on.

Finally you will need macrame cord. If you want you can buy the satin macrame cord. This is very easy to work with for a beginner. But, you can also use twine, string, cord, rope, jute, or rug yarn. The yarn that is sold for use in gift wrapping is also perfect. This is available in many colors and for only 50¢ you can buy 6 yards. When you are cutting your macrame cord, make it about 5 times longer than you want your completed piece.

To begin, start with the easy macrame knots that follow. These are the basic knots used in macrame. All other knots are a variation of these. Once you can do these easy knots you will be ready for some of the variations.

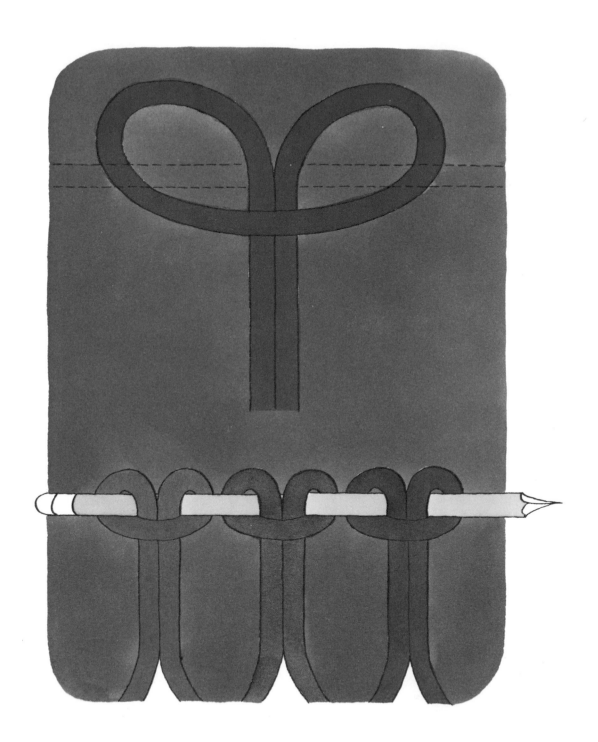

EASY
MACRAME

The first knot we will learn is the LARK'S HEAD KNOT. Take one cord. Fold it in half. Now let the top fall forward making a loop. Slip a pencil in back of the two cords, through the loops. Pull the two cords tight. You will use this knot to put your macrame cords on your holding cord or stick. Practice making the LARK'S HEAD KNOT. If you want, use a pencil for your holding stick.

Now let's try a HALF HITCH. Begin by putting your cord on the holding stick with the LARK'S HEAD KNOT. Let the cord on the left hang. Take your right cord and put it over the left one. Bring it around the back of the left cord and then bring it back over to form a loop around the left cord. Now tighten by pulling both cords. Practice making HALF HITCHES. If you make several Half Hitch knots on the same cord, it is called a Half Hitch Sinnet. A sinnet is a group of knots exactly the same in a row. A DOUBLE HALF HITCH is made by closing the Half Hitch Knot twice on the same side.

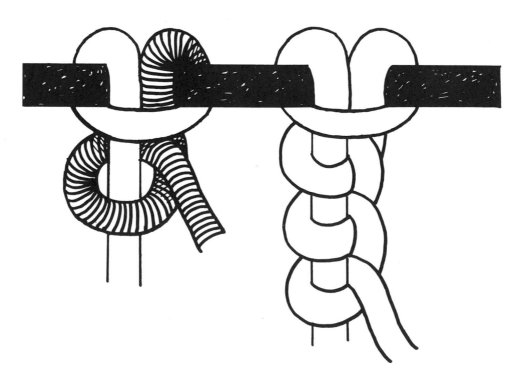

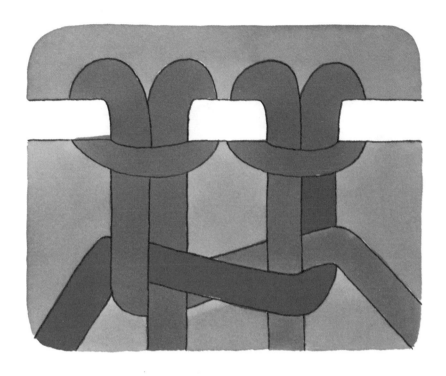

The HALF KNOT uses the first four cords. You will use the left and right cords only. The middle cords are filler cords. Take the cord on the right. Put it over the filler cords. Then, under the left cord. Now take the left cord and put it under the filler cords. Pull it over the top of the loop on the right. Now pull the knot tight. Practice the HALF KNOT. This will also be used for the SQUARE KNOT.

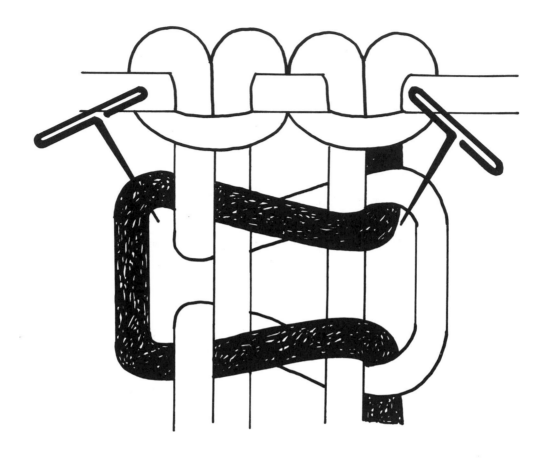

To make a SQUARE KNOT, begin by making a HALF KNOT. Then, take the cord that is now on the right side. Put it under the filler cords and over the cord on the left side. Now take the cord on the left and put it over the filler cords. Then pull it through the loop on the right side. Now tighten the SQUARE KNOT. Since this knot is a little harder than the others, practice this for a while longer. Make SQUARE KNOT SINNETS.

When you have practiced these knots and are able to do each one without following the illustrations or directions you will be ready to have fun with some easy macrame projects.

EASY PROJECTS
A Macrame Belt

You can have a lot of fun making a macrame belt. You will need:

    T Pins

    A foam rubber pillow

    2 Rings for loops

    4 Cords that are 6 yards long

> (A very easy and pretty belt can be made by using the yarn Gift Tye. You can buy 6 yards for 50¢. If you use this gift tye you will not have to cut your cords.)

Begin your belt by attaching each cord to the rings with the LARK'S HEAD KNOT. Now do a HALF HITCH. Pin each cord to your pillow. Put the pin through the HALF HITCH KNOT.

The next row across do a SQUARE KNOT.

Now on this row leave the two cords on the left side hang free. Then make a SQUARE KNOT using the next four cords.

On the next row, begin your SQUARE KNOT at the left as you did on the second row. This is known as ALTERNATE SQUARE KNOTS. Pin your knots to the pillow as you go. Pin about every third knot.

Now continue with the ALTERNATE SQUARE KNOTS until your belt is the correct length to go around your waist. When you have reached the correct length, secure each cord using a HALF HITCH. Leave the ends hang free.

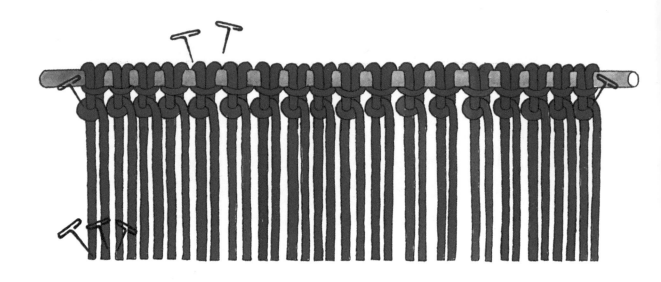

A Wall Hanging

Another fun way to use the knots you know is to make a wall hanging. Here is an easy wall hanging for you to start with.

You will need:

A stick (for the frame)

18 Cords that are each 4 yards long

T Pins

Foam rubber pillow

Attach each cord using the LARK'S HEAD KNOT to the stick.

Do the next row across in the HALF HITCH KNOT. Now pin each cord to your pillow.

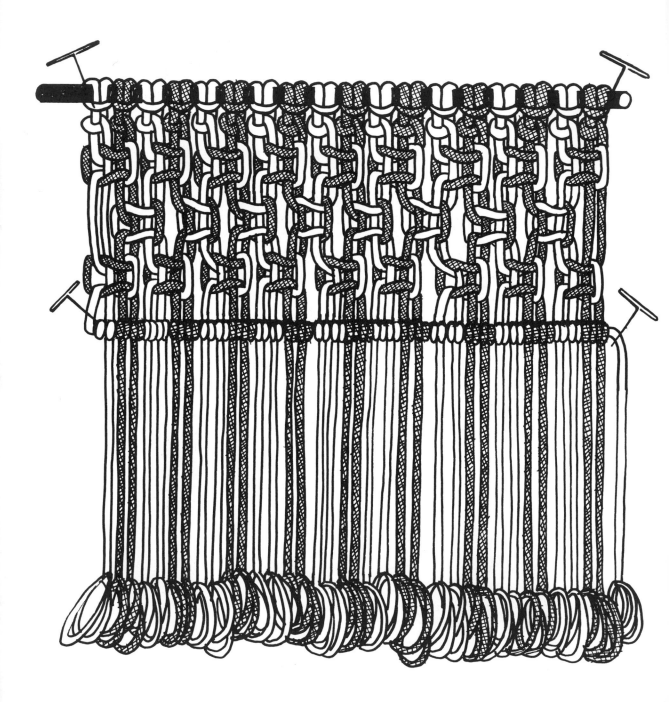

Do the next 6 rows in the ALTERNATE SQUARE KNOT. Pin these down.

When you finish the sixth row of ALTERNATE SQUARE KNOTS, begin the next row in a HORIZONTAL DOUBLE HALF HITCH. To do this, pull the first cord on the left completely across your wall hanging. Pin this to the pillow. Then, work each cord in a double HALF HITCH over this cord. When you have done each cord this way, remove the pin from the filler cord. It will now be on the right side of your wall hanging.

Do 10 rows of SQUARE KNOT SINNETS.
Remember, a sinnet is when you do the same knot.
This is different than ALTERNATE SQUARE KNOTS.

When you have your 10 rows completed, pin
them down. Then, do the next 6 rows in the
ALTERNATE SQUARE KNOT. Pin down.

26

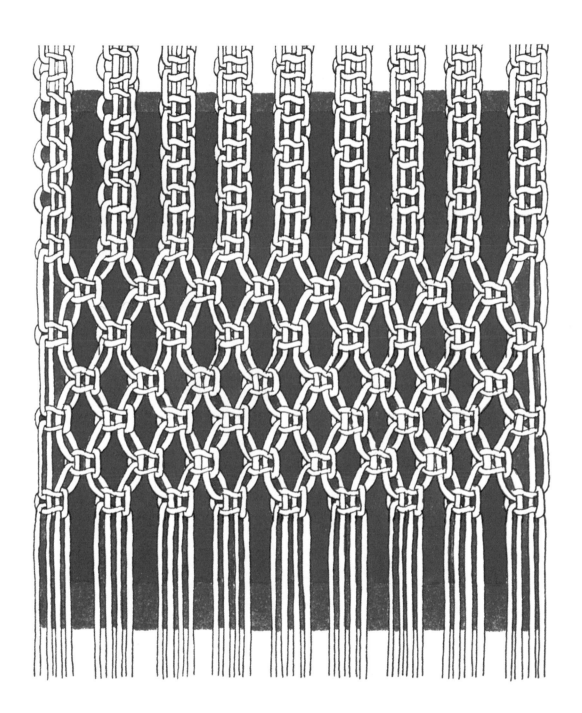

Now, do another HORIZONTAL HALF HITCH. Again, take the first cord on the left and pull it across the wall hanging. Pin to the pillow.

Do 10 more rows of SQUARE KNOT SINNETS. Then, secure each cord with a HALF HITCH. Now, trim the fringe on the loose ends so that they are all even.

To hang your wall hanging, take a cord that is 14 to 16 inches long. Use a vertical HALF HITCH to fasten each end to the stick.

Now your wall hanging is ready to display.

Have fun making these wall hangings for gifts. If you use the yarn gift tye you will have many colors that you can make wall hangings in.

Once you have made several belts and several wall hangings you will be ready to try some of the variations. Macrame your gifts and you will not only have some very nice gifts but macrame is one way you can have fun in your spare time.

31

how to have fun

creative
craft
books